SiZE WiSE

BUSTER BOOKS

Written by Camilla de la Bedoyere
Illustrated by Vasilisa Romanenko

Edited by Susannah Bailey
Designed by Zoe Bradley
Cover design by Angie Allison

First published in Great Britain in 2023 by Buster Books,
9 Lion Yard, Tremadoc Road, London SW4 7NQ

 www.mombooks.com/buster  Buster Books 🐦 @BusterBooks 📷 @buster_books

A CIP catalogue record for this book is available from the British Library.

ISBN: 978-1-78055-824-0

2 4 6 8 10 9 7 5 3 1

This book was printed in August 2023 by
Shenzhen Wing King Tong Paper Products Co. Ltd.,
Shenzhen, Guangdong, China.

CONTENTS

Introduction   8
Down in the Deep   10
Built Like a Tank   14
The Secrets of Sand   16
Little vs Large   18
Patterned Shells   22
Ocean Soup   24
Night Flight   26
Flying Jewels   30
Stunning Seeds   32
Colossal Blossom   34
Going Underground   38
Lots of Frogs   40
Tiny vs Tough   42
Big Ears   46
Rainbow Diatoms   48
Here Be Dragons   50
Mini Mariners   54
Hovering Hummers   56
Flapping Bats   58
Hunter in the Cold   60
Eggstremely Small   64
Reach for the Sky   66
Remarkable Rodents   68
Hungry Fungi   72
Big Beak   74
Sparkling Crystals   76
Flutter By, Butterfly   80
A Giant of a Spider   82
It's Jumbo!   84
Beetle Collection   88
Silent Killer   90
Glossary, Units of Measurement   92
and Imperial Measurements

INTRODUCTION

Big or small, mega or micro – size matters here on Earth.

In this book, you will learn lots about the miniscule and massive things and creatures that live on our planet. Nearly all the beautiful illustrations are shown at life-size with accurate measurements, meaning you will get a real sense of the amazing size and scale of the natural world.

Discover the biggest flower in the world, the enormous eye of a colossal squid, and the surprisingly large ears of a dinky fennec fox. Compare your hand to that of a silverback gorilla, an eagle owl's sharp talons and a tiger's mighty paw to get an awe-inspiring sense of these animals' strength and power. You will find huge mushrooms and giant beetles that are bigger than your foot. And beware the monster-sized spider and venomous viper – they can be terrifying at their real size!

The world of tiny things is also shown here, and you will be able to see them both life-size and zoomed in. Explore an almost invisible world of seeds and snowflakes, with their exquisite patterns and shapes. Dive into the ocean to find microscopic animals and plants and dig into the soil to see the marvellous mini-beasts that lurk beneath our feet.

Make sure to look out for two symbols – a ⊕ to show that a picture has been zoomed in, and a ⊖ to show that a picture has been zoomed out. Both of these mean the particular images shown are not at life-size. You will also see pictures that compare humans to natural things or animals. There is a glossary at the back of the book containing helpful words, in case you don't understand something, along with information about measurements.

Enjoy your journey through an extraordinary world of big and small size-related facts and get wise to the size of all things.

DOWN IN THE DEEP

The colossal squid has the largest eyes of any animal currently known. They are possibly even the largest eyes that have ever existed in the animal kingdom, including those of the dinosaurs. They measure about 27 centimetres across – roughly the size of a football. In comparison, a human eye is only 2.2 cm across.

COLOSSAL SQUID EYE

HUMAN EYE

SEEING IN THE DARK

A colossal squid's eyes, as well as being ginormous, also have built-in headlights that help them see in the dark. These headlights are called 'photophores'. When their eyes turn inwards to focus on objects directly in front of their arms and tentacles, the photophores provide enough light for the squid to see its prey.

WHY SO HUGE?

Colossal squid live in very deep ocean waters, at about 1,000 metres below the sea surface, where sunlight does not reach. They need large pupils to help them see in the dark ocean depths. Human eyes can only detect light to a depth of around 500–600 m.

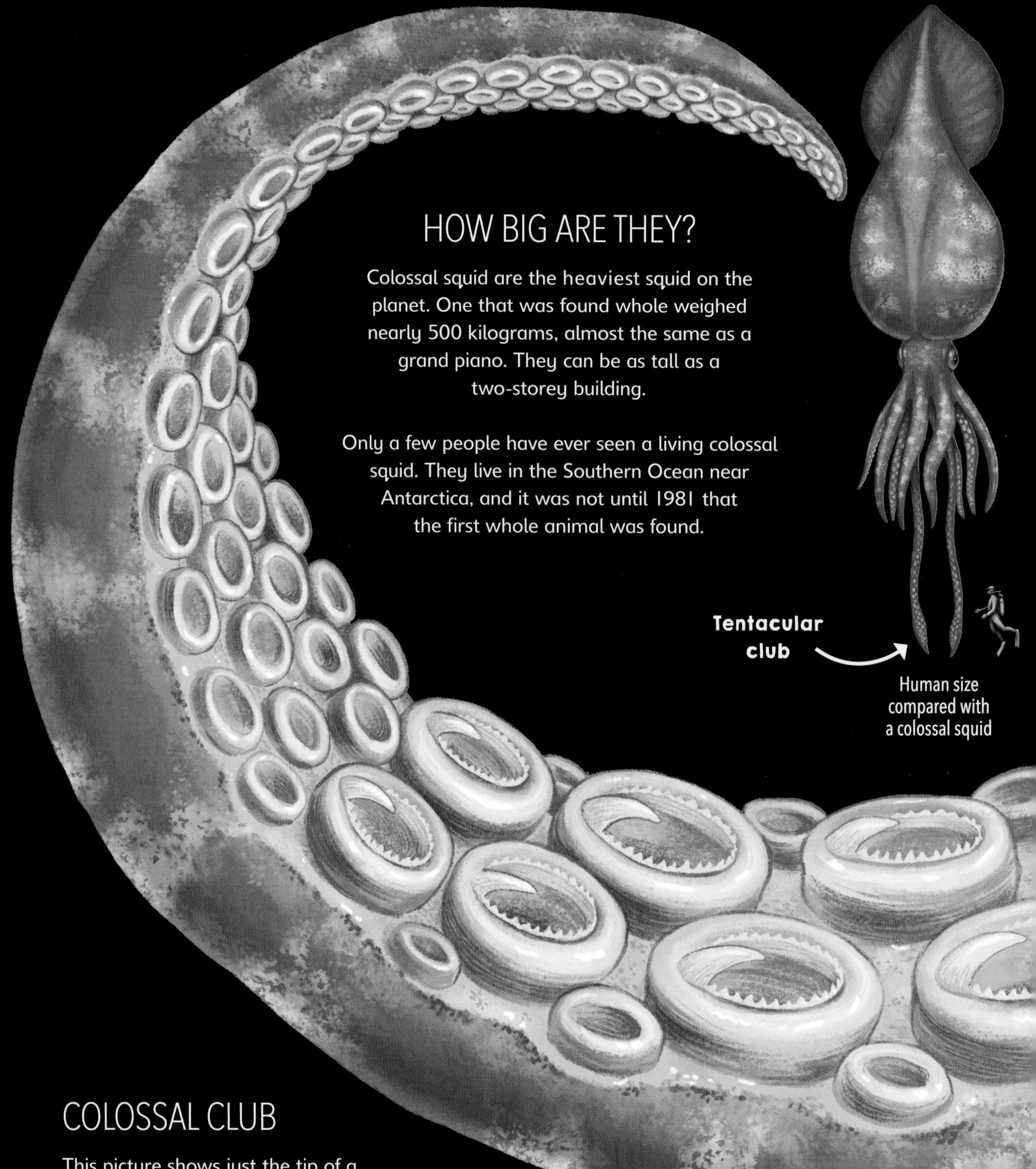

HOW BIG ARE THEY?

Colossal squid are the heaviest squid on the planet. One that was found whole weighed nearly 500 kilograms, almost the same as a grand piano. They can be as tall as a two-storey building.

Only a few people have ever seen a living colossal squid. They live in the Southern Ocean near Antarctica, and it was not until 1981 that the first whole animal was found.

Tentacular club

Human size compared with a colossal squid

COLOSSAL CLUB

This picture shows just the tip of a colossal squid's 'tentacular club'. The whole club measures in at 85 cm long – that's half the height of an adult human.

HUNTING TIME

Huge eyes are excellent for spotting prey, but how does a colossal squid catch it? With its terrifying tentacles, of course ...

The inside surfaces of the arms and tentacles of a squid are lined with hundreds of suction cups, which are 2–5 cm in diameter.

HOLD ON

The squid's suction cups are lined with rings of 'chitin', a sharp material, and terrifying hooks. Both these features help the squid attach to, and keep hold of, its prey, with the hooks even rotating for extra grip. Scientists sometimes find circular scars from these suckers on the heads of sperm whales.

Chitin

Hook

BUILT LIKE A TANK

Tortoises have slowly roamed the Earth for at least 200 million years. Giant tortoises can grow up to 1.4 m long and weigh 300 kg or more – that's the same as more than 1,000 padloper tortoises, the smallest members of the family. Whatever its size and weight, a tortoise is built like an armoured tank. Its tough, bony shell protects the soft body inside so well that these slow-moving reptiles rarely need to run from danger.

Human size compared with a giant tortoise

THE GIANT TORTOISE

Giant tortoises reach a height of 70 cm. They may be able to grow bigger than this, but no one knows for sure. Giant tortoises are now very rare, after being hunted for centuries, but it's possible that, if left alone on their island homes, they could reach the great age of 200 or more.

A tortoise's shell is mostly bone and covered in tough plates, called scutes. The tall dome shape of the shell is difficult for a predator to bite into.

GIANT TORTOISE

THE PADLOPER TORTOISE

The world's smallest tortoises are not much bigger than a mouse, at just 7–8 cm long. The padloper tortoise is so small that even birds can attack it. Male padloper tortoises are smaller than the females and may only reach 6 cm long.

SPECKLED PADLOPER TORTOISE

THE SECRETS OF SAND

No one normally notices tiny specks of sand, which range in size from 0.05 millimetres to 2 millimetres. Even when you're stepping on them at the seaside, or running handfuls through your fingertips, you probably don't stare at them really closely. Until now ...

GRAINS OF SAND,
life-size at 2 mm

WHERE DOES SAND COME FROM?

Sand is made up of grains – tiny, loose pieces of minerals, rock and soil. These grains are formed when rocks from cliffs and mountains are broken down, often by water and wind, over a long period of time. They are then blown or washed down to the coasts. Another type of sand comes from living organisms. When living things die, the ocean slowly wears down their shells and skeletons into tiny sand particles.

ZOOM IN

When you put sand under a powerful microscope, it can start to look a lot more interesting. It may include coral, shells, gemstones or even bits of volcanic rock. Sand is made up of its environment, so what you see will change a lot depending on where it's found. And just as every beach is different, all grains of sand will be different from each other.

CORAL

These are just some of the miniscule things that can be seen in a handful of sand at a tropical beach in Maui, Hawaii. The sand there is made up of rocks, corals and shells. At this size, the particles have been magnified under a microscope by approximately 300 times.

ROCK

SHELL

LITTLE VS LARGE

The first dinosaurs lived about 245 million years ago and these land-living reptiles went on to evolve into an incredible variety of shapes and sizes. The largest carnivorous dinosaur was probably *Tyrannosaurus rex* – a colossal beast that weighed up to 7 tonnes and could, despite its size, still chase prey at an impressive speed of 40 km per hour. At the other end of the scale was the tiny *Parvicursor*, a fast-moving, two-legged predator that weighed 500 grams – that's less than a chicken weighs!

TINY PARVICURSOR

Being mini has its advantages. Small dinosaurs were able to dart around in the undergrowth, hiding from predators and ambushing their prey. *Parvicursor* belonged to a group of dinosaurs called alvarezsaurs that ran on two long, strong legs. *Parvicursor* was one of the smallest of the dinosaurs, probably measuring 40 cm from beak to tail, based on the proportions of its known relatives.

PARVICURSOR

A long tail balanced *Parvicursor* as it ran, and anchored the strong running muscles of its hind leg.

HISTORY'S MYSTERY

Dinosaurs died out about 66 million years ago – so it is difficult to know exactly what they looked like and how they lived. The alvarezsaurs belong to one of the most mysterious groups yet discovered. They were unusually small, had beak-like mouths and narrow skulls, like modern birds, but their arms were short and stubby with a single claw on each one. The claws may have been used for digging bugs out of the ground or killing prey ... but no one really knows.

Little is known about *Parvicursor* because few fossils have been discovered. A fossilized thighbone discovered in Mongolia measures just 5 cm.

It had a horn-shaped claw on each arm that measured about 1–2 cm.

Its long legs were perfect for running at speed.

TERRIFYING T. REX

Tyrannosaurus rex was possibly the largest land animal that survived purely on a diet of meat. It needed to eat about 111 kg of food a day, and could put on about 15 kg in weight every week!

With giant teeth and a bite that was strong enough to crush bone, it was a fearsome killer. It stood at 13 m long – that's longer and heavier than a bus. Its huge head alone was 1.5 m long and its jaw contained about 50 teeth. Some of the teeth, including their roots, were the size of bananas!

Turn over to see those teeth at life-size ...

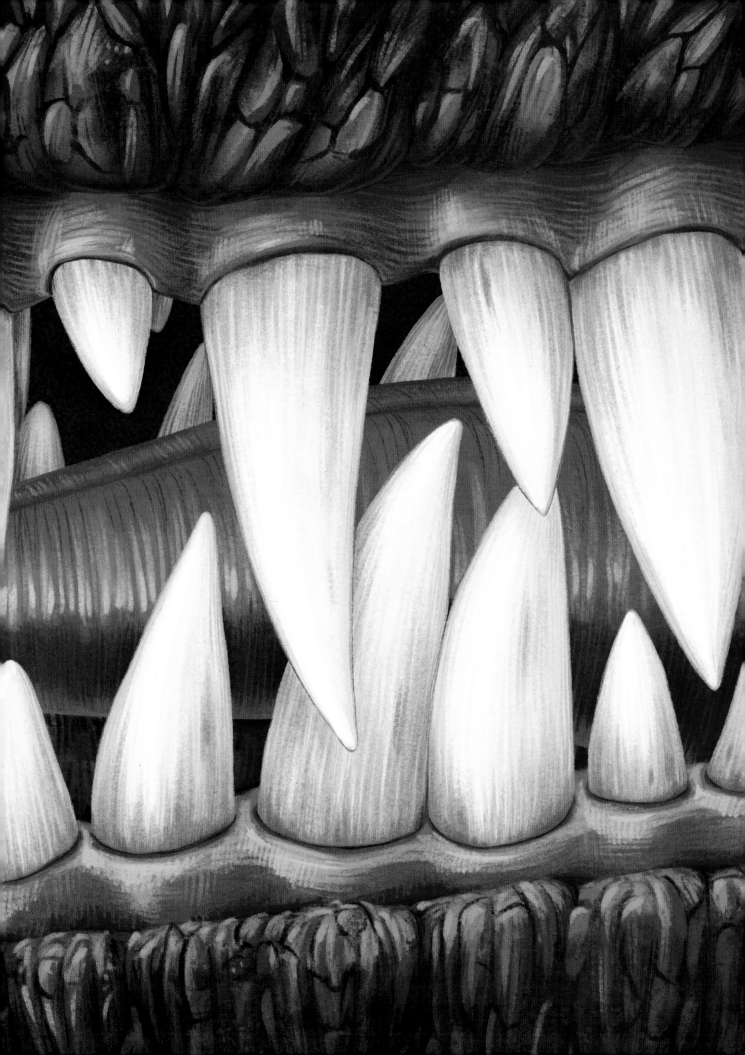

PATTERNED SHELLS

Some animals, especially those in the group called molluscs, grow a hard covering, or shell, to protect their soft bodies. The shells we find at the beach are usually empty – when the animal dies its shell gets washed up on to the shore. Some animals have just one shell, others have two and some, such as hermit crabs, have no shells of their own but temporarily use the empty shells of other creatures.

GIANT LAND SNAIL

LARGEST ON THE LAND

Giant land snails have shells that grow 20 cm long. They are so big you need two hands to hold one.

TRUMPET CONCH

The largest shell, called the trumpet conch or Australian trumpet, belongs to an Australian sea snail. One record-breaking specimen measured 77 cm long and 1.1 m around its widest part. It weighed 18 kg when alive.

Human size compared with a trumpet conch

TRUMPET CONCH SHELL (TIP)

LEOPARD CONE SHELL

CONE SHELLS

The largest cone shell is the leopard cone shell – it can grow up to 16 cm long. However, whether they are little or large, all cone shells hide a deadly secret. They contain snails that can fire venom-tipped darts. These deliver a lethal dose of poison to their prey, which are usually fish or other small sea creatures. The venom of some species is so powerful that it can kill a human within minutes.

OCEAN SOUP

The world's five oceans connect together in one vast, moving mass of water. It is the largest habitat in the entire universe (that we know about, anyway), but most of the things that live in it are smaller than your fingernail.

ZOEAS

These tiny creatures look like aliens, but they are actually young crabs.

TINY PLANKTON

The smallest living things found in the oceans are called plankton. While many of them can move, they are all too weak or little to fight the strong ocean currents that flow around the globe, carrying these lifeforms with them. Plankton includes algae, microscopic organisms and the tiny young of much larger adult creatures. Oceans contain billions upon billions of plankton. They are an important source of food for many other marine creatures. Here is a small selection of them. Lots are too miniscule to see properly, so these pictures have been zoomed in to help you take a proper look.

ZOEA,
life-size at 1 mm

BLUE BUTTON,
life-size at 3 cm

BLUE BUTTONS

These bizarre creatures are actually a group of soft-bodied animals that belong to the jellyfish family. They float in the water and use stingers on their tentacles to catch prey.

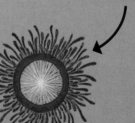

ANTARCTIC KRILL

Related to shrimp and crabs, these animals live in the cold Southern Ocean around Antarctica. Many marine animals, including whales, feast on vast swarms of krill there.

ANTARCTIC KRILL,
life-size at 5 cm

RADIOLARIA

Most radiolaria are round-shaped organisms with long spines that help them to float. The majority of them cannot be seen without a microscope.

RADIOLARIA,
life-size at 1-2 mm

COPEPODS

Copepods are very common – they make up as much as 70% of all animal plankton. They have T-shaped bodies and limbs for swimming.

COPEPOD,
life-size at 1-2 mm

DINOFLAGELLATE,
life-size at 2 mm

DINOFLAGELLATES

Dinoflagellates are organisms that, like plants, can use sunlight, water and air to make their own food. This dinoflagellate is called a sea sparkle because it creates a blue-green light that twinkles at night.

GREEN ALGAE,
too small to show life-size

GREEN ALGAE

Microscopic green algae are usually made of just one cell. They are too small to see with the naked eye, although they often clump together to make a group. Large green algae are called seaweed.

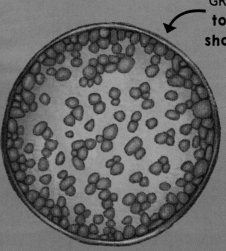

NIGHT FLIGHT

There are about 220 species of owl. The world's largest owl is the Eurasian eagle owl, while the smallest species is the elf owl. Owls are supreme hunters, owing their success to their ability to take prey by surprise, hunting in silence and almost total darkness. As it swoops, an owl's soft, fluffy feathers muffle the sound of beating wings and its eyes, being forward-facing and unusually large for a bird, can collect a large amount of light and allow the owl to accurately judge distance.

EURASIAN EAGLE OWL

After sunset, a Eurasian eagle owl perches high in a tree, or on a cliff-top, and its deep 'uhu-uhu-uhu' hoots can be heard far and wide. That's why this bird is also called the uhu owl! It's the world's largest owl and its bulky frame creates a dark silhouette against the night sky. Female Eurasian eagle owls are bigger than males, with a length of up to 75 cm. They weigh about 4 kg and have a wingspan of 2 m, which is taller than the height of most humans.

An owl's eyes are so large that it can't move them and must twist its entire head when it wants to see to the side or behind.

NIGHT HUNTERS

Most owls are nocturnal and roost in trees during the day, where their speckled plumage of brown, cream and black feathers helps to camouflage them. Owls hunt small creatures such as mice but, thanks to their size and strength, Eurasian eagle owls can catch bigger prey, including hares, foxes and young deer. They even hunt other big birds, such as hawks and falcons.

HIDDEN EARS

The tufts of feathers on the owl's head add to its height, but they are not ears. An owl's ears are holes on the sides of its head and hidden beneath its feathers. These birds have superb hearing, and they can pinpoint the sound of a small animal moving on the ground, even while flying above it.

ELF OWL

The tiniest known owls, elf owls are found in North and Central America. You could easily fit one inside your pocket. At just 12 cm tall, an elf owl is one-sixth of the height of a Eurasian eagle owl. It weighs no more than 55 g – that's less than a tennis ball. These little owls are too small to fight off large predators, such as hawks and snakes, but up to four of them may gang up together to defend themselves from an attacker.

ELF OWL

Eurasian eagle owl talons

HOME SWEET HOME

Owls do not build nests like most other birds. They either lay their eggs in abandoned nests, or they use ready-made homes such as tree holes. Elf owls sometimes nest in cacti, laying their eggs in holes that were originally made by gila woodpeckers for their own nests. Nesting inside a cactus is sensible as the plant's prickly spines prevent predators reaching the owl's eggs and chicks. Eurasian eagle owls lay their eggs in other birds' abandoned nests, or on ledges, clifftops or even on the ground.

The legs and feet of the Eurasian eagle owl are coated in feathers to keep them warm.

SHARP TALONS

Owls have four toes on each foot. When they fly, three toes face forwards and one faces back. When it is perching, or grabbing prey, an owl can swivel one toe backwards and it is used, like a thumb, to grip.

Eurasian eagle owls have massive feet – measuring more than 15 cm across – with piercing claws, or talons, which need to be strong enough to grip hold of a struggling mammal. Elf owls, however, mostly eat insects and scorpions, which they catch using their feet or their beak, so their feet are small and weak by comparison. Their feet measure about 2–3 cm across.

The underside of an owl's foot is rough and knobbly, so it doesn't slip on a perch or lose grip of its prey.

FLYING JEWELS

Dragonflies are large flying insects that dart and dive with incredible speed and agility as they chase other bugs to eat. They are among the largest of all insects and are equipped with enormous eyes that help them to find their prey.

THE GIANT PETALTAIL

The largest dragonfly species alive today is thought to be the giant petaltail, from Australia. It has a wingspan of 16 cm and a body length of 12.5 cm.

GIANT PETALTAIL

A dragonfly's big eyes wrap around its head, allowing it to see in all directions. This means it can spot predators behind it while also looking for food.

BIG-EYED BEASTIES

Dragonflies have the largest eyes of any insect alive today, covering most of the head like a pair of enormous goggles. A human eye has one lens, which focuses light in the eyeball to create an image in the brain. A dragonfly's eye can have up to 30,000 lenses. Together they make a mosaic of thousands of images in the insect's brain to create a moving picture of shapes and colours.

MEGANEURA

THE MEGANEURA

Some of the largest insects to ever live flew
through prehistoric skies 300 million years ago.
Meganeura, a cousin of modern dragonflies, had a
wingspan of over 65 cm. That's bigger than many
birds of prey! Meganeura could grow to this great
size because the climate at the time was warmer
than today and contained more oxygen.

Meganeura belonged to a group of bugs called
griffinflies. It lived a similar life to modern
dragonflies although, thanks to its huge size,
it could have preyed on bigger animals
such as the first frog-like creatures.

**Dragonflies hold
the bug world
record for fast flying,
with top speeds of
58 km per hour being
measured for one
Australian species.**

STUNNING SEEDS

A tiny seed is the first stage in the life of a plant. Just add warmth, water, air and sunshine to see it grow. Here are a selection of extraordinary seeds. Some of the pictures are zoomed in to reveal their intricate shapes and patterns.

MILKWEED SEED, **life-size at 6–8 mm**

SEEDS ON THE MOVE

Seeds grow best when they can get away from their parent plant and do not compete with them for light and water. There are many ways that seeds travel – they may float away in water, fly through the air, move with the help of animals – or even explode from their pods!

MINI PARACHUTES

The smallest seeds travel by air – this is called wind dispersal. Some, such as dandelion and milkweed seeds, have special structures that work like parachutes to lift them from their parent plant and carry them away. Most seeds land within a few metres of the parent plant, but sometimes they glide for a kilometre or more.

DANDELION SEED, **life-size at 3 mm**

ORCHID SEEDS 🔍

The smallest seeds are made by orchids – tropical plants with exotic, colourful flowers. They have a very thin outer layer (a seed coat) with an embryo inside. The tiniest of all orchid seeds are just 85 micrometres long – that is 0.008 mm. The largest are 6 mm. Orchid seeds are as light as dust and float, invisibly, in the wind. Three million orchid seeds together weigh just 1 g.

ORCHID SEED,
**life-size at
1 mm**

🔍 CORNFLOWER SEEDS

Cornflower seeds have a tuft of hairs on their tops that absorb water and swell. As they dry, the hairs shrink again. A cycle of swelling and shrinking causes the tuft to push the seed along the ground, like a broom, helping its dispersal. Ants also help disperse the seeds by burying them underground.

CORNFLOWER SEED,
life-size at 3–4 mm

WILD CARROT SEEDS 🔍

The seeds of wild carrot plants are oval-shaped and covered in tiny hook-like spikes. Many seeds have hooks that help them attach to passing animals, which then carry the seeds to a new place where they can grow.

WILD CARROT SEED,
life-size at 3–4 mm

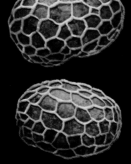

POPPY SEED,
life-size at 1 mm

🔍 POPPY SEEDS

Like many seeds that are dispersed by wind, poppy seeds have honeycomb patterns on the surfaces of their seed coats. These beautiful structures create air spaces, which help the seeds travel when the wind shakes them loose from the seed pod in which they grew.

COLOSSAL BLOSSOM

The world's smallest flowers grow on plants that live in ponds and are tinier than the full stop at the end of this sentence. The biggest flowers, however, are massive blooms that can weigh up to 7 kg. These Rafflesia blooms, found in Southeast Asia, grow to widths of up to 1 m and are found on the rainforest floor, in the dappled shade of tall trees.

PARASITE PLANT

Rafflesia has no roots, leaves or stem and, instead of growing in the soil, it grows on the stems of a vine plant. This means it is a parasite, an organism that grows on another organism. It sucks the nutrients out of this vine rather than making its own food. Its lifecycle begins when a bump suddenly appears on the vine's woody bark and slowly grows bigger ... It is preparing for an explosive appearance that will thrill plant-lovers and scientists all over the world.

BLOOMING MARVELLOUS

The bloom stays in bud for about nine months before suddenly opening up, like a giant cabbage, with five leathery petals covered in white spots. At its centre is a deep, cup-shaped hole that is lined with spikes. At first, the flower has the delicate smell of mushrooms, but after four days the odour turns foul and smells like rotting fish or meat.

Rafflesia flowers look and smell this way to tempt flies to visit them. The flies are hoping to find somewhere to lay their eggs. As they crawl into its dark, smelly centre, they pollinate the flower – which can then grow hundreds of thousands of tiny seeds.

RAFFLESIA FLOWER ♀

JUNGLE GIANTS

Many plants grow big in rainforests. Some leaves grow so large that orangutans can use them as umbrellas. The tallest rainforest trees measure more than 100 m – that's as tall as a skyscraper building. Rainforest trees can grow this big because there is plenty of rainfall and sunlight above the canopy – things that they use to make food and grow.

Rafflesia is unusual because it grows on the gloomy forest floor where there is little sunlight. However, it has an endless supply of food from its host plant – the vine – so it can just keep growing and growing and growing ...

Turn over to see a section of it life-size ...

→

GOING UNDERGROUND

Soil, the top layer of soft, crumbly material that forms on the surface of land, is the magical place where plants can grow, and where billions of tiny things live. It is made up of water, organic material (stuff that is alive, or was alive) and inorganic material (everything else, including sand and stones). Here is a selection of what's living in it.

WORMS

Most earthworms grow no bigger than a finger, although some types can grow more than 30 cm long. An earthworm has five hearts but no eyes – its super-sensitive skin detects light instead and it is also used to breathe and taste.

PSEUDOSCORPIONS 🔍

Like spiders and scorpions, a pseudoscorpion is a member of the arachnid family; its name means false-scorpion. The largest ones only reach 1 cm long, unlike other arachnids, which can reach 30 cm in length. Pseudoscorpions have long venomous pincers which they use to attack other soil creatures.

PSEUDOSCORPION,
life-size
at 2 mm

SLUGS

Common garden slugs can grow huge in size. The great grey slug, or leopard slug (named after its striking spotted appearance), can grow up to 20 cm in size. These slugs are omnivores and so will eat everything – including other slugs.

SPRINGTAIL,
**life-size
at 1 mm**

🔍 SPRINGTAILS

Up to 100,000 garden springtails are thought to live in a cubic metre of soil – but these little bugs are rarely noticed. That's because they are silent, secretive and very small. They can run to escape trouble, or even leap into the air. Springtails have round, colourful bodies, six legs and often measure less than 1 mm long.

WATER BEARS 🔍

At 0.3–1.2 mm long, tardigrades, or water bears, are among the world's smallest and toughest animals, with sharp, curved claws and dagger-like teeth. Water bears love damp soil and are so small they can squeeze between two touching grains of sand.

WATER BEAR,
**life-size
at 1 mm**

LOTS OF FROGS

Frogs are amphibians – vertebrates with smooth, moist skin that lay eggs, usually in water. Most frogs could sit comfortably in your hand, but not the Goliath frog. This mighty monster lives in West Africa and it is the world's largest frog, measuring 30 times longer than the smallest frogs, most of which live in the Americas.

GOLIATH FROG

THE GOLIATH FROG

Named after a Biblical giant, the Goliath frog can grow to 30 cm long, although one record-breaking specimen was 36.8 cm. With its legs stretched out, it actually measured a colossal 87.6 cm! These frogs are heavy too: they can weigh as much as a human baby, with maximum weights of around 3.6 kg.

POISON-ARROW FROGS

Many frogs make a poison in their skin that makes them taste bad, so predators won't want to eat them. Tiny frogs that live in the Amazon Rainforest, often called poison-arrow frogs, can be only 2.5 cm in size but their poison is so deadly that a single drop could be enough to kill a human. They have very colourful skin, to warn predators not to try eating them.

POISON-ARROW FROGS

MICRO FROGS 🔍

The smallest frogs are less than 10 mm long. Most of them, such as the Cuban frog and gold frog, live in Central and South America, but the tiniest frog, *Paedophryne amauensis*, has recently been discovered in Papua New Guinea, where it hides in leaf litter on the forest floor. At just 7 mm long, it may even be the smallest vertebrate in the world.

PAEDOPHRYNE AMAUENSIS, **life-size at 7 mm**

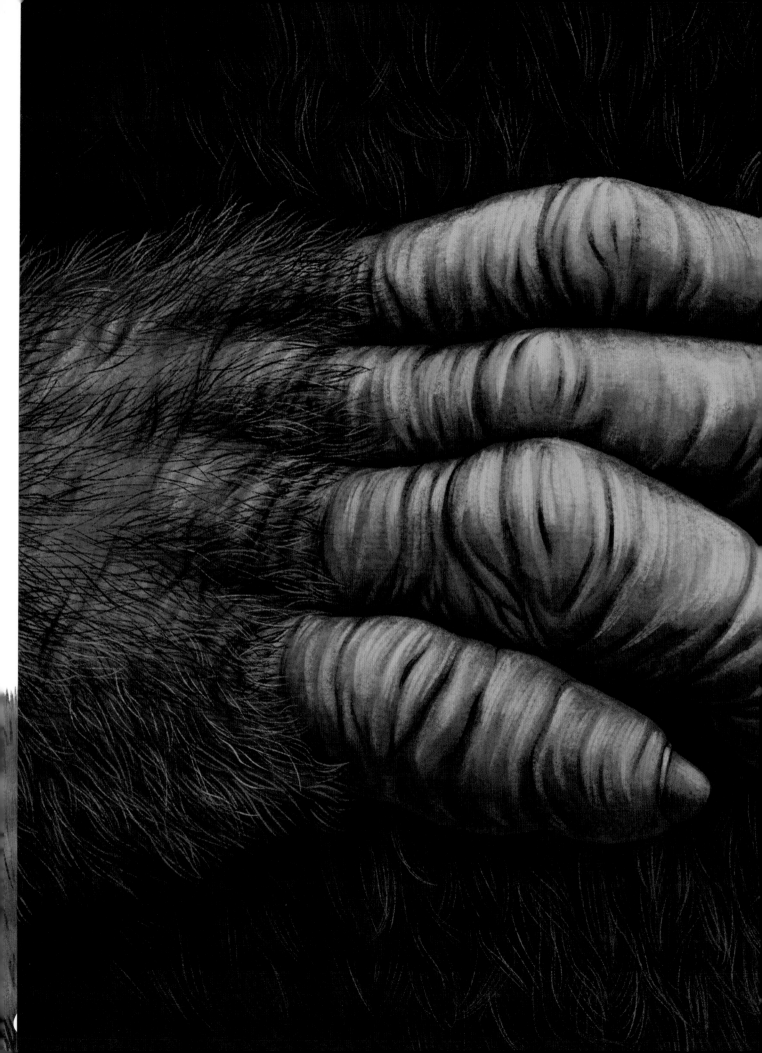

BIG EARS

The Sahara Desert is one of the world's most extreme habitats. With searing heat in the daytime, precious little water and not much food, few animals choose to make a hot desert like this their home. Those that do, such as the little fennec fox, work hard to survive and have some smart strategies to help them cope.

THE FENNEC FOX

The fennec fox looks as if it is wearing the ears of a much larger animal. At 15 cm long, they are the largest ears, in relation to body size, of any meat-eating creature.

It is not just the smallest fox in the world, it is the smallest member of the wild dog family. With a weight of just 1 kg – a fifth of the weight of a pet cat – it would take 80 fennec foxes to weigh the same as a grey wolf, which is the largest member of the dog family. The smallest fennec foxes measure 24 cm long, with a tail of 18 cm. Fennec foxes are just 19 cm tall, measured from the ground to the shoulder.

DESERT SURVIVORS

Big ears help fennec foxes to lose heat. Warm blood rushes to the ears, which are full of blood vessels. The heat escapes through the thin skin of the ears, and the foxes cool down.

Fennec foxes avoid the heat by spending most of the day hidden in underground dens. Their thick fur keeps them warm on cold nights but also protects their skin from the strong Sun. Their paws are covered in fluffy fur so they don't burn on hot sand.

A baby fennec fox is called a kit. It is blind and pure white when born and weighs just 50 g – about the same as a slice of bread.

SUPER SENSE

Enormous ears are also handy for listening. Fennec foxes have superb hearing. They can hear the quiet noises made by beetles and tiny termites as they burrow through the sand beneath the fox's feet.

FENNEC FOX

RAINBOW DIATOMS

Diatoms are microscopic green algae (plants) that can be found in water and come in all shapes and sizes. The smallest ones are only two thousandths of a millimetre big. No one knows how many species of diatom live in oceans and rivers, but there may be as many as 2 million different types. Even though most diatoms are far too small to see, we've zoomed in on some species here so you can learn their names, and look at their amazing colours and forms.

ETHMODISCUS REX

A huge seawater diatom.

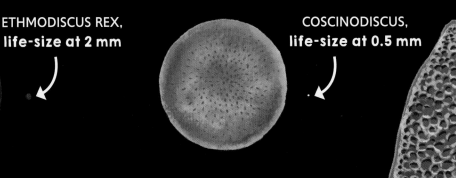

ETHMODISCUS REX, life-size at 2 mm

COSCINODISCUS

One of the largest diatoms.

COSCINODISCUS, life-size at 0.5 mm

DIDYMOSPHENIA GEMINATA

The largest freshwater diatom species measures, at the most, 0.1 mm long and 0.04 mm wide.

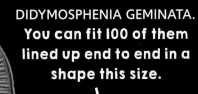

DIDYMOSPHENIA GEMINATA.
You can fit 100 of them lined up end to end in a shape this size.

STEPHANOPYXIS

ACTINOCYCLUS

ASTERIONELLA

SMALL BUT MIGHTY

Diatoms may be tiny, but they are important. They live as part of the ocean plankton and in freshwater habitats, and are an essential source of food for animals there. Diatoms use sunlight to make food and to grow, and as they do this they make oxygen – the gas we breathe. They also remove carbon dioxide from the air. That's the gas that is contributing to the problem of climate change. So these creatures are mini superheroes in the fight against global warming.

TRICERATIUM

GLASS HOUSES

Each diatom is just one cell big, but they sometimes live together in groups, called colonies. Their cell walls are made of silica, the same mineral that is used to make glass. When sunlight passes through silica it can split into different colours, turning these tiny creatures into rainbow jewels of the sea.

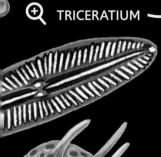

CAMPYLODISCUS

FRUSTULIA

HERE BE DRAGONS

Long ago, explorers wrote the warning 'Here be dragons' on maps of remote places. Perhaps those early travellers had reached the Komodo island in Southeast Asia, where the world's largest lizards prowl. These lizards may not spit fire, but they are still called dragons and, like their mythical namesakes, they are big, bold and deadly. The smallest lizards are not so scary. Barely larger than a sunflower seed, nano chameleons survive on a diet of tiny mites and wingless insects called springtails.

KOMODO DRAGONS

Male Komodos can grow to an impressive 3 m long – as long as a small car – and have big, bulky bodies that weigh up to 100 kg. Female dragons are smaller, rarely reaching more than 2.4 m long and weighing in at 40 kg. Komodo dragons have short but powerful legs and a massive tail.

TASTING THE AIR

Like other lizards, a Komodo dragon uses its tongue to smell. The tongue is forked, and the foul stench of rotting flesh is its favourite smell. Komodo dragons will eat carrion (the dead remains of animals) as well as the live animals they hunt.

AMBUSH!

Thanks to their great size and strength, the largest Komodo dragons can hunt deer, pigs and goats, but sometimes they attack humans, too. A hungry Komodo dragon lurks in the shadows, waiting for its prey to walk nearby, then – silently but swiftly – it ambushes the victim. As the predator bites, it releases venom in its saliva, which oozes into the puncture wound and eventually kills the prey.

KOMODO DRAGON

An adult Komodo
dragon has a big
appetite, and can eat
80% of its body weight
in just one meal. That's
like you eating 256
bananas in one go.

SUIT OF ARMOUR

Reptile skin is covered in scales that are made of keratin, which is a tough material that is also found in fingernails, feathers and hooves. Komodo dragons, however, have an extra layer of protection – a sheet of small bony plates, called 'osteoderms', that lies beneath the scales. The dragons have few natural enemies (except each other). Males dragons battle at mating time, but the osteoderms fit together like chain mail and in places they are almost impossible to penetrate, protecting the lizards from all but the worst attacks.

Human size compared with a Komodo dragon

Komodo dragon claw

FIERCE CLAWS

Komodo dragons usually attack with their teeth – which measure up to 2 cm long – and sometimes with their clawed feet, too. Each foot has five toes with a long, curved, sharp claw on each one. These powerful feet are most useful for digging dens, where the lizards like to hide out on the hottest days, or for digging nests where females lay their eggs.

NANO CHAMELEONS

Which lizard can claim to be the world's smallest? No one knows for sure because tiny lizards are almost impossible to find, and they move so fast they are hard to catch, too. The dwarf gecko is just 32 mm long, including its tail, and the pygmy chameleon is not much bigger, at about 35 mm long. In 2021, another teeny-tiny lizard was discovered – the nano chameleon. Its total length is also about 35 mm but its body is smaller than either of its close contenders – making it the current champion of little lizards!

NANO CHAMELEON

MINI MARINERS

Seen from space, the oceans turn Earth into a blue planet that is full of life. Peer beneath the waves and you'll find that oceans are a wonderful mixture of seawater and billions of tiny creatures that float, swim or dive into the inky darkness far below. Small animals that drift along on marine currents are called zooplankton, but others are big and strong enough to choose their own direction of travel.

LIGHT AND DARK

The oceans cover 68% of the Earth's surface. Near the water's surface, sunlight powers photosynthesis, the process by which plants and algae grow and become food for animals. At a depth of about 200 m, sunlight begins to disappear and ocean water soon turns pitch-black, creating a world of darkness that can extend to breath-taking depths of 10,000 m. Sunlit or inky-dark, these habitats are home to an unimaginable number and variety of tiny animals.

BOX JELLYFISH

At 1–2 cm wide, these tiny jellyfish may be the smallest in the world, but their stings pack a painful punch. There are about 25 species of box jellyfish that deliver a nasty dose of venom from stingers on their tentacles and their transparent bell. People can get stung when warm water currents sweep the jellyfish close to shore.

BOX JELLYFISH

PYGMY OCTOPUS

The largest octopuses can have an arm span of 9 m, while the smallest ones have bodies that are just 1–2 cm long and an arm span of 5 cm. All octopuses have eight arms that are covered in suckers.

PYGMY OCTOPUS

PYGMY SEAHORSE

Pygmy seahorses are tiny and very well camouflaged. They grow to a maximum length of 2.4 cm and live on colourful coral. Their bodies are covered in lumps and bumps that match the coral's surface and they also match the coral's colour, which is usually purple and pink or yellow and orange. Unusually, male seahorses look after the female's eggs in a pouch on their body, releasing them when the babies – called fry – are big enough to survive on their own. A newborn pygmy seahorse fry is just 2 mm long.

PYGMY SEAHORSE

SPIKEFIN GOBY

At just 2–3 cm long, the spikefin goby is one of the world's smallest fish that lives around coral. It relishes life in the sunlit waters of warm seas around Australia and Southeast Asia. The long spines on its fins help the goby defend itself from attack by bigger fish.

SPIKEFIN GOBY

PYGMY SQUID

Pygmy squid are the size of a thumbnail, so they are almost impossible to spot in the sea. Despite having a body length of just 1.6 cm, these tentacled terrors attack fish and shrimp that are twice their size, using a deadly venom to kill their prey.

PYGMY SQUID

DWARF LANTERNSHARK

Believed to be the world's smallest shark, the dwarf lanternshark is about 10 cm long at birth and grows to 20 cm long. Its body is lined with light-making cells called 'photophores'. Lanternsharks light up their bodies to help them hunt in the twilight waters.

DWARF LANTERNSHARK

HOVERING HUMMERS

The smallest bird in the world is a hummingbird – the bee hummingbird. It belongs to a family of dazzling birds that are often rainbow-coloured and are affectionately called 'hummers' after the buzzing, humming sound their wings make when they hover at flowers to feed. At just 20 g, even the largest species of hummingbird, the giant hummingbird, weighs less than four grapes.

MALE BEE HUMMINGBIRD

THE BEE HUMMINGBIRD

Half of this bird's length is made up of beak and tail, so its actual body is not much bigger than an acorn. Females reach about 6 cm in length, but males are smaller at about 5.5 cm. A male bee hummingbird weighs under 2 g – a little more than a paperclip. Like other hummingbirds, it has to spend much of its time finding food to fuel its energetic flying, visiting 1,500 flowers a day.

NUT-SIZED NESTS

It's no surprise that the world's smallest birds build the smallest nests, with widths of just 2.5 cm. They are usually cup-shaped and made of moss and bark, which is held together by threads of sticky silk taken from spiders. A female bee hummingbird lays one or two eggs in her nest. The miniature chicks are blind and bald when they hatch, but quickly grow and can fly from the nest when they are barely a month old.

FEMALE BEE HUMMINGBIRD **in her nest**

SWORD-BILLED HUMMINGBIRD

One of the world's largest hummingbirds, the sword-billed hummingbird, has the longest beak – relative to its size – of any bird. This hummingbird is 17–23 cm long, with the beak measuring up to 10 cm. The beak can even be longer than the bird's body (excluding the tail). It uses its beak and its long tongue to reach deep into tubular-shaped flowers where the nectar is found, and to pick dead bugs out of spiders' webs.

SWORD-BILLED HUMMINGBIRD

MINI EGGS

The smallest bird egg is the size of a chickpea and is laid by the vervain hummingbird. At less than 1 cm long, it weighs just 0.4 g. Experts believe there may be even smaller bird eggs waiting to be discovered – the problem is some species of hummingbird have eggs and nests that are so small and well hidden that no one has ever seen them!

VERVAIN
HUMMINGBIRD
with her egg

FLAPPING BATS

The forests of Southeast Asia are home to both the world's largest and smallest bats. These peculiar creatures have furry bodies and leathery wings and hang upside down by their feet when they want to rest. While some mammals can soar between trees, bats are the only ones that can truly fly.

THE BUMBLEBEE BAT

The smallest bat and smallest mammal in the world is the bumblebee bat. It lives in caves in Southeast Asia.

When an adult bumblebee bat spreads its wings, they span around 15 cm, but its head and body are just 3 cm long. It hunts insects in the dark, so this bat uses its sense of hearing to find its prey. That's why it needs such large ears. Its ears can measure one-third of the bat's body length – that's like us having ears that are bigger than our head. A bumblebee bat weighs just 2 g – about the same as two peanuts.

BUMBLEEBEE BAT

A bat's wings are made of leathery skin and are supported by a framework of extremely long arm and finger bones.

THE FLYING FOX BAT

The world's largest bats belong to a group called flying foxes because they have big eyes, fox-like ears and long snouts. The gigantic Indian flying fox is likely the biggest bat of all, with a wingspan of 1.7 m or more, roughly ten times bigger than the wingspan of the smallest bat. Its head-body length can exceed 23 cm and its weight can reach 1.6 kg. The largest flying fox would weigh about the same as 800 bumblebee bats.

INDIAN FLYING FOX BAT

NIGHT AND DAY

While most small bats are nocturnal hunters of insects, flying foxes are fruit eaters and are active in the day as well as at night. They hang from trees, cloaked by their black wings as they rest, then suddenly take to the air. Flapping their huge wings, the bats soar through the sky, searching for food.

HUNTER IN THE COLD

An awesome predator, the Siberian tiger prowls through a world of shadow and snow. The biggest member of the cat family, a male Siberian tiger can measure 3.3 m from its nose to the tip of its tail. Its weight may even exceed 350 kg – that is equivalent to the weight of 70 pet cats. Also known as Amur tigers, these striped killers live in China and Russia.

SIBERIAN TIGER

A DEADLY PREDATOR

Packed with muscles and coated in thick fur to protect it from the cold, this deadly predator moves with grace and stealth but can burst from its hiding place to ambush its prey with fatal speed and strength. When a tiger chases its prey it can reach speeds of 20 m per second, in short bursts, before pouncing. Tigers can kill and drag animals that are far larger than themselves – even deer, oxen or bears that are four times heavier than they are. When hungry, this tiger can eat around 27 kg of food in one night.

A thick mane of fur around the tiger's neck and fluffy, furry paws help to keep the chills away when winter temperatures drop to −40°C.

Rarely seen, this
tiger's huge pawprints
or its mighty roar are
often the only clues
that it lurks nearby –
watching and waiting.

PAWS FOR THOUGHT

Tigers have two obvious sets of weapons: dagger-like canine teeth that can measure 4 cm long and a set of clawed paws. A male Siberian tiger's paw pad measures 14.5 cm wide and a one-year-old male cub can have paws that are already bigger than his mother's! As dusk falls, tigers become more active and prepare to hunt. Their razor-sharp claws are essential for pinning prey to the ground, and a mighty bite to the victim's neck delivers a swift end.

THE BIG CATS

There are 38 species of wild cat in the world today, but only four of them are 'big cats' that can roar: tigers, lions, leopards and jaguars. Small and medium-sized cats, such as pumas, cheetahs and lynx, cannot roar, but they do purr – just like pet cats.

SIBERIAN TIGER PAW

Toe pads help to muffle the sound of a tiger as it stalks its prey.

TIGERS AT RISK

There are five types, or sub-species, of tiger alive today and they are all endangered. Their survival is threatened by the loss of their habitats and by humans hunting them. It is thought there are fewer than 500 wild Siberian tigers left – and the number may be as low as 270.

Human size compared with a Siberian tiger

Tigers have retractable claws, which means they can be tucked away and protected by a cover of skin when not in use.

EGGSTREMELY SMALL

More than 99% of all animals that have ever lived on Earth began life by hatching out of eggs. These little capsules contain all the ingredients needed to begin a creature's life story as it starts to grow. Insects have been around for at least 300 million years, and in that time their miniscule eggs have evolved to survive in all sorts of environments. The ones here are so tiny that they are best seen with a microscope. Zoomed in, they come alive in a variety of fun details and shapes.

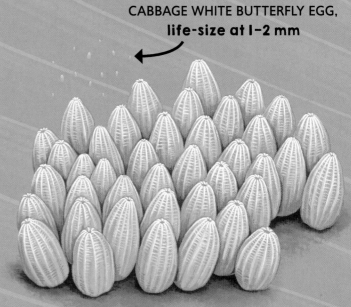

CABBAGE WHITE BUTTERFLY EGG,
life-size at 1-2 mm

CABBAGE WHITE BUTTERFLY

Each egg of a cabbage white butterfly looks like a cob of corn. Like many insect eggs, they are normally laid on the underside of a leaf, hidden from egg-stealing predators.

HARLEQUIN BUG EGG,
life-size at 1.3 mm

HARLEQUIN BUGS

When harlequin bug eggs are first laid, they are pale yellow, but they quickly develop into stacks of white cylinders beautifully decorated with thick black stripes. When the bugs hatch, the lids open and little bug nymphs emerge.

SPINED SOLDIERS

Eggs are often wrapped in a tough outer coating, or shell, to stop them from drying out. The spiky shells of these spined soldier bug eggs also deter animals from trying to eat them.

SPINED SOLDIER BUG EGG,
life-size at 1 mm

BLUE MORPHO BUTTERFLIES 🔍

When a blue morpho's bright-green egg develops a red band it's a sign that it has been fertilized, and will eventually become one of the world's biggest and most beautiful butterflies.

STICK INSECT EGG,
life-size at 2 mm

BLUE MORPHO EGG,
life-size at 1–2 mm

STICK INSECTS 🔍

Eggs are tasty, so it is a good idea to disguise them from predators. Stick insects lay eggs with interesting markings that look like dried seeds to trick the wasps that usually eat the eggs into leaving them alone.

SHIELD BUG EGG,
life-size at 1.5 mm

SHIELD BUGS 🔍

These smiley-faced eggs belong to a shield bug. The 'mouth' is actually a little crack in the egg that will open up when the young bug is ready to hatch.

REACH FOR THE SKY

When a baby giraffe is born it falls 2 m (the height from its mother's body) to the ground, but it can stand and walk just 20 minutes later. It's already 2 m tall! In a few years' time it will be one of the tallest creatures on the planet – with the longest neck.

MASAI GIRAFFES

There are four types of giraffe, with Masai bull (male) giraffes being the tallest. One record-breaker reached 6.1 m tall, although heights of about 5 m are more normal, which is still as big as a two-storey house. Despite the impressive length of a giraffe's neck, it still has just seven neck bones – the same number of neck bones as most mammals.

The distance between a giraffe's lungs and its vocal chords – at the top of its neck – is so great that these gangly grazers can't make loud or high-pitched noises. However, they can grunt and hum.

BIG BABY

A newborn giraffe weighs 50 kg – the same as about 17 newborn human babies – and drinking 6 litres of milk a day helps it grow fast. By the time it's an adult, a giraffe will have feet with a hoof diameter of 25–30 cm (the size of dinner plates) and an appetite to match. Giraffes spend most of the day eating, using their tall necks to reach the sweetest leaves at the top of the tree, where other animals cannot reach. Its legs are so long – about 2 m – that, despite having the world's longest neck, a giraffe cannot drink water from the ground without spreading its legs wide or bending its knees first.

At 2.4 m long, this is the longest neck of any living animal.

Giraffes look gangly and heavy, but they can run at speeds of 56 km per hour, with their necks swaying from side to side as they gallop.

MASAI GIRAFFE

A giraffe's head is only about 60 cm long, roughly a quarter of the size of its neck. If us humans had the same proportions we'd have necks around 90 cm long, about nine times as long as your neck is now.

Human size compared with a Masai giraffe

67

REMARKABLE RODENTS

There are about 2,370 species, or types, of rodent in the world – that's more than 40% of all mammals. Most of them are mice and rats, so they're small enough to fit in your hand. In general, rodents have little furry bodies with four legs, whiskers, a long tail and extra-long incisor teeth for gnawing.

PYGMY JERBOA

PYGMY JERBOA

The smallest rodent is the pygmy jerboa, which lives in Pakistan. Its furry body is just 4 cm long. A jerboa uses its enormous feet for jumping – at 2 cm long they are huge for such a small creature. If a human had such big feet, they would be a whopping 90 cm long.

Jumping jerboas can leap an impressive 3 m in a single bound – that's 75 times their body length. Some types of jerboa can also jump up to heights of 1 m when they are trying to escape predators, such as snakes.

A jerboa's hind legs are at least four times longer than its front legs. Its tail is twice the length of its body.

Three million years ago, there were mega-rodents. The size and weight of a bull, these giant rat-like animals may have used their big teeth to fight sabre-toothed cats.

DIGGING DOWN

A jerboa uses its front paws to dig long, deep burrows, where it hides or shelters from extreme cold and heat. Each burrow can be up to 2 m deep and more than 50 cm long.

CAPYBARA

The world's largest living rodent is the capybara, reaching up to 1.4 m wide. It can stand 66 cm tall at the shoulder and weigh 66 kg. Despite its great size and some impressive front teeth, this modern giant of the rodent world is a gentle, shy creature.

A capybara looks a bit like an overgrown guinea pig. Its eyes and ears are at the top of its head – perfect for an animal that loves to swim. Capybaras use their webbed feet to paddle in the wetlands of South America.

Capybaras have been called 'nature's chairs' as they are so big and gentle that animals, especially birds, are happy to rest on them.

CAPYBARA

GROWING TEETH

A rodent's front teeth, or incisors, never stop getting bigger. A capybara's incisors can grow to more than 4 cm long, which means one tooth can be bigger than a pygmy jerboa.

Human size compared with a capybara

Turn over to see the capybara's head at life-size ...

HUNGRY FUNGI

Mushrooms, toadstools, yeast, moulds, mildews and rust are all types of fungi. These bizarre organisms are often mistaken for plants, but they are actually more closely related to animals, as they must find food and absorb it, just like animals do. Fungi live almost everywhere on Earth: in the air, the soil and in water. However, most of them are tiny and live in the soil, making them almost invisible. Therefore, some of the ones you see here have been zoomed in, to help you see their bright colours and fascinating shapes better.

SUPER SPORES

Mushrooms and toadstools are the parts of a fungus that we most often see. The mushroom caps are called fruiting bodies, as they grow spores, a type of seed. The lower side of a mushroom cap is made up of many paper-thin layers, called gills, where the spores grow.

Cap

FLY AGARIC

FLY AGARIC

Probably the most recognizable mushroom thanks to its bright colouring, the fly agaric can grow up to 20 cm across and 30 cm tall. Despite their tempting appearance, these fungi are toxic to humans, although other creatures, such as slugs and red squirrels, do enjoy feasting on them.

Gills

BAKER'S YEAST

This fungus lives as single cells that can grow new cells by dividing in two. It is used to make bread rise.

BAKER'S YEAST, **too small to show life-size**

MUCOR MOULD

Also known as black fungus, this mould lives in the soil but it also grows on food, such as bread. When the ripe spores are released they are so small they can float in the air.

MUCOR MOULD, **too small to show life-size**

MINI MUSHROOMS

One of the world's smallest mushrooms – the nut fungus – grows on acorns and beechnuts. Its cap is just 1–4 mm wide, so it is similar in size to the more colourful Bisporella mushroom, which grows on rotting wood.

NUT FUNGUS

BISPORELLA MUSHROOM

PENICILLIUM

This is a microscopic mould that is used to make penicillin, a medicine that treats infections caused by bacteria.

PENICILLIUM, **too small to show life-size**

CANDLESNUFF FUNGUS

The 'stalks' on a candlesnuff fungus grow up to 6 cm tall, so you can see them with the naked eye if you look carefully. They feed on dead or rotting trees, producing chemicals which break down the wood into nutrients. Some of these nutrients are returned to the soil where they help new trees to grow.

CANDLESNUFF FUNGUS

BIG BEAK

With their enormous beaks, toucans look as if they could topple over. A toco toucan, for example, has a beak that makes up one-third of its entire length – growing between 16–23 cm long. So why does this tropical bird need such a colourful, over-sized mouth?

Maxilla (upper beak)

TOCO TOUCAN

Mandible (lower beak)

BEAK BENEFITS

A toucan can use its long beak to reach the juicy fruits growing at its tip, where other birds cannot reach. A long beak is also perfect for reaching deep into a tree hole and picking up bugs.

The beak looks heavy – but it isn't because it's full of air holes, like a sponge or foam. This thick foam layer makes the beak unusually bulky, but it helps build strength into the structure so it doesn't bend or break.

HEATING UP

Tropical forests where toucans live can get hot and steamy, but big beaks keep birds cool. A toucan's beak is full of blood vessels. If the bird gets too warm, blood flows around the beak and quickly loses heat thanks to the beak's large surface area. Little beaks have a smaller surface area, so big-beaked birds are definitely cooler.

SHOW-OFFS

A toco toucan's strong, long beak with a bold, orange-red colour tells other toucans that the bird is fit and healthy, and would make a great mate. The blue skin around its eyes and brightly coloured beak help it recognize members of its family.

Groups of toucans live together in the forest, where the trees often grow thick and tall. When they can't find each other, the birds make croaking calls and loudly clack their beaks to say, 'I'm over here!'. Large beaks are particularly good at making loud sounds that travel further.

SPARKLING CRYSTALS

Ice, salt and sugar all exist as crystals – incredible forms with regular shapes that often glint and glimmer with colour and light. The snowflake is an example of a beautiful crystal. The smallest crystals are less than one-thousandth of a millimetre, so special equipment is needed to see them in a laboratory.

WHAT IS A CRYSTAL?

Everything on Earth is made up of matter. Matter is made up of miniscule building blocks called atoms, which join together to make molecules. The atoms and molecules in solids are mostly arranged in regular patterns that make three-dimensional shapes, such as crystals. The smooth side of a crystal is called a face and the shape it takes is called its 'habit'.

TINY CRYSTALS

The smallest water crystals are called microcrystals ('micro' means small). They form when water gets cold and, at their smallest, they contain just 275 molecules of water. Most snow crystals are based on a hexagon shape, which means they have six sides or points. The biggest snowflakes form when the ice crystals freeze, melt and refreeze.

SNOWFLAKE

FALLING FLAKES

As the ice crystals fall through the clouds, they clump together, forming larger flakes. These larger flakes are called 'aggregates', and they often simply look like lumps of frozen water. They are rarely the perfect shapes we imagine when thinking of snowflakes.

SNOWFLAKE, life-size at 5 mm

SNOWFLAKE, life-size at 0.5 mm

SNOWFLAKE, life-size at 5 cm

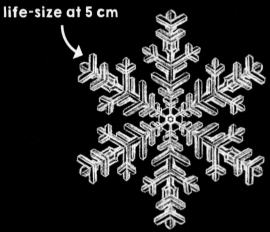

In 1887, it was reported that a giant snowflake measuring 38 cm in diameter and 20 cm thick fell on the ground. It would have been approximately this size.

77

SALT CRYSTALS

If you look at common salt under a microscope you will see that it is made up of many tiny crystals, each the shape of a cube. This is the salt that we put on our food and it's a solid mineral called halite, or sodium chloride.

Seawater is salty because it has sodium chloride dissolved in it, as well as other types of salt. If the salts from all of the oceans were spread out over the land, there would be a layer more than 150 m thick.

WHY IS SALT WHITE?

When seen under a microscope, salt crystals are colourless and transparent – which means they are see-through. So why does a pile of salt look brilliant white? That's because when light passes through the crystals, the light rays – which are white – are scattered around all of the crystals before bouncing right out again to our eyes, making the salt appear white to us.

SALT CRYSTAL,
life-size at 1 mm

🔍 HOPPER SALT CRYSTALS

When salt crystals form very slowly they can, in certain conditions, take on a beautiful crystal shape called a hopper. The edges of each hopper crystal grow much faster than its middle, which ends up looking hollow, or sunken. Hopper salt dissolves more easily than regular salt, which means it tastes saltier.

🔍 SUGAR CRYSTALS

Sugar is a type of food that plants make, using the energy in sunlight. We then extract it from the plant. When sugar is mixed with hot water it dissolves, meaning we can't see it, but it is still there and creates a sweet solution, or syrup. If sugary syrup is left to dry out, over several days, the sugar turns into a pile of tiny, shiny crystals. This is called white sugar, and we use it in baking or add it to foods to make them sweeter.

· · · · · · · · · · · · · · · ·
Sugar crystals form in a shape called a hexagonal prism.
· · · · · · · · · · · · · · · ·

SUGAR CRYSTAL,
life-size at 1 mm

FLUTTER BY, BUTTERFLY

A Queen Alexandra's birdwing is the biggest known butterfly in the world. Females have a wingspan of 28 cm and weigh 25 g – that's around the same size as the span of two adult hands held together. These butterflies are very rare. They live in just one small area of forest in Papua New Guinea, a tropical island country in the Pacific Ocean. One of these spectacular insects weighs the same as 2,500 of its smallest cousin – the dwarf blue butterfly.

QUEEN ALEXANDRA'S BIRDWING

Once a caterpillar has hatched from its tiny egg it has one job to do: eat! When it's fully grown, a Queen Alexandra's birdwing caterpillar will measure nearly 12 cm long and 3 cm in diameter. Caterpillars eat plants and may increase in size more than 2,000 times before they turn into adults – that's like a human baby growing to the size of a bus.

THE DWARF BLUE BUTTERFLY.
It has a wingspan of just 14 mm and weighs 10 milligrams.

COLOUR COMBINATIONS

The female Queen Alexandra's birdwing has brown-black colours with white patches that help it to blend into the dappled shadows of the forest. Males flash their more colourful wings in special courtship dances to attract females at mating time.

Dwarf blues are mostly a dull brown colour with patches that camouflage them, helping them avoid attack from predators such as birds or lizards.

QUEEN ALEXANDRA'S BIRDWING CATERPILLAR.
The red prickles warn predators that this caterpillar has toxic flesh.

HOME SWEET HOME

Large butterflies are more common in woodlands and forests, while smaller species often prefer meadows and fields. Queen Alexandra's birdwings live in tropical forests, and like to flutter beneath the forest's cooler leafy canopy. Dwarf blues are very active butterflies, flitting between flowers in the open grasslands of South Africa and Zimbabwe.

A GIANT OF A SPIDER

Whether it is big or itsy-bitsy, a spider is fast, hungry and hairy! Meet a miniscule eight-legged arachnid and a Goliath bird-eating spider, a monstrous predator with mighty fangs. These giant South American arachnids are the world's heaviest spiders and have body sizes up to around 12 cm. They live on the leafy forest floor of mountain rainforests, where they hide in burrows or under rocks.

GOLIATH BIRD-EATING SPIDER

GOLIATH SPIDER

This spider is named after Goliath, a Biblical giant. Although they are big enough to eat birds, and therefore are called bird-eating spiders, these arachnids usually eat insects, other spiders and occasionally mice, frogs, snakes and lizards.

PET MONSTER

Female spiders are usually larger than the males and this species is no exception. The largest known Goliath bird-eating spider was a pet, called Rosi. She lived to the age of 12 years and her body (not including her legs) measured 11.9 cm. She eventually weighed 175 g, which is the same as 600 garden spiders.

Although this looks like a leg, it is actually a 'pedipalp'. Spiders use these like antennae, helping them sense objects they encounter.

PATU DIGUA SPIDER ⊕

The smallest spiders in the world all measure less than half a millimetre wide, including their legs. That's smaller than a pinhead. One mini midget spider of the *Patu digua* species was found to have a body that measured just 0.15 mm – which is almost invisible to the naked eye. Midget spiders' silken webs are about 1 cm wide.

PATU DIGUA, **too small to show life-size**

A fang measures
2 cm long and
injects venom,
which is said to
be no more
painful than a
wasp's sting.

HAIRY HISSERS

When a Goliath bird-eating spider is
scared, it hisses loudly and rubs the hairy
bristles on its front legs (and pedipalps) as
a warning sign. Next, it waves its first two
pairs of legs at the attacker and raises its
huge fangs so they are ready to plunge
and bite. Micro spiders, like *Patu digua*,
also hunt their prey. They are believed to
attack other spiders, using their venomous
jaws to bite and kill them.

IT'S JUMBO!

The world's biggest land animal is an African elephant. Measuring 4 m tall and weighing up to 12 t, the males are colossal beasts with huge feet to carry that heavy load. African elephants also lay claim to having the biggest ears of any animal, the longest noses, huge appetites and very big babies!

ENORMOUS EARS

The biggest mammals easily overheat. An elephant solves that problem by having huge ears. As the elephant flaps them in the breeze, blood rushes into the wide, flat outer ears and cools its blood by a whopping 19°C. Big bodies also need plenty of food, and the largest elephants can spend 18 hours a day eating, putting away 200 kg of food and drinking 200 L of water.

HANDY NOSE

An elephant's trunk is a 2-m-long nose that ends in sensitive, finger-like tips. It's packed with about 150,000 mini-muscles that allow it to push, pull, grip, carry and gently stroke. An elephant can use its trunk to suck up to 9 L of water at a time – and either pour it into its mouth, or spray it everywhere!

An elephant's tusks are teeth made from ivory. The longest tusk ever measured was 3.49 m long.

Human size compared with an African elephant

WHAT'S IN A NAME?

Jumbo the African elephant was born in 1860, captured and put into a travelling circus. He measured around 4 m tall and his great size impressed many people who saw him across Europe and the United States. His name was soon used to describe anything that was extra big, and we still use the word 'jumbo' today.

AFRICAN ELEPHANT ♀

BIG FOOT

An elephant's foot can be as much as 50 cm across. You'd need a piece of string 1.6 m long to measure all around the outer edge (the foot's circumference). As an elephant walks, its feet spread out to absorb the weight and fatty pads help to cushion the impact.

Feet aren't just handy for walking – elephants also use them to listen! These beasts communicate over long distance by making deep, low rumbling sounds that travel through the ground. Far away, other elephants 'hear' the noise through their feet.

Turn over to see a foot at life-size ...

→

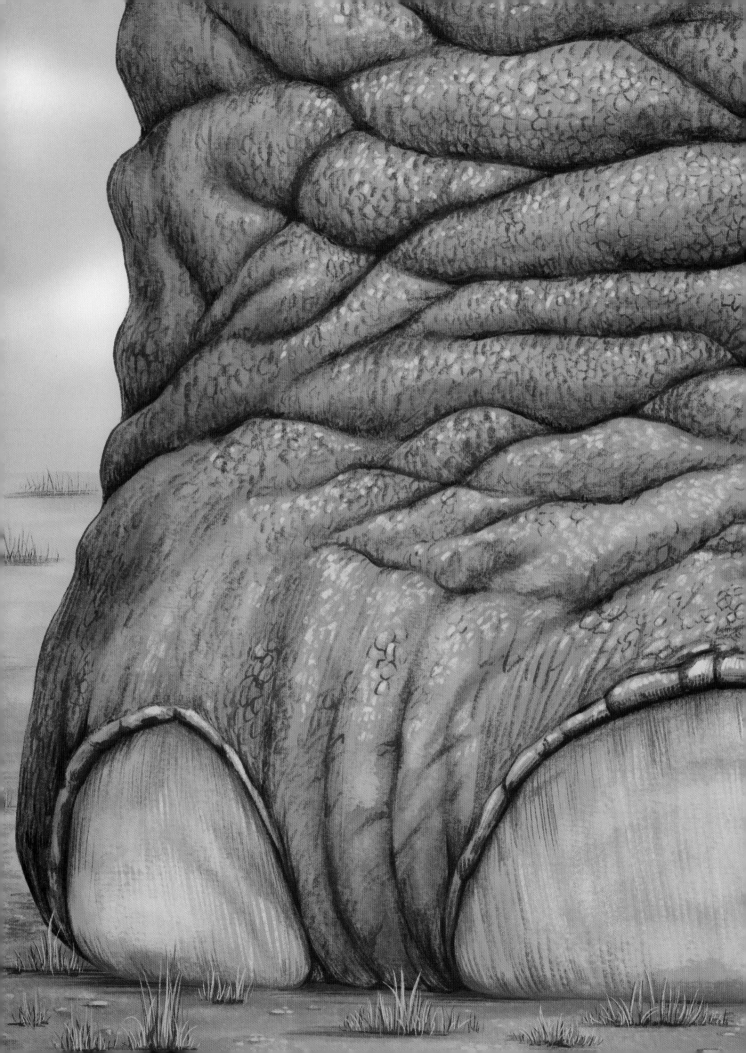

BEETLE COLLECTION

Beetles are incredible insects that can be both amazingly big or absolutely tiny. With at least 360,000 different species of beetle in the world, they are the largest group of insects. The secret of their success lies in their ability to take the basic beetle body plan and adapt it to almost any lifestyle.

WHAT ARE BEETLES?

Like other insects, beetles have six legs and a body that is divided into three sections: head, thorax (middle) and abdomen. They fly using one pair of wings with another pair that folds over them, like a case, for protection. Beetles lay eggs that hatch into grubs, or larvae, which look very different from the adults.

HERCULES BEETLE

HERCULES BEETLE

Hercules beetles are the longest horned beetles. Males use these horns to fight with each other over potential mates. The beetles can reach an impressive 17 cm in length and weigh up to 50 g, but they have mighty larvae, too. The soft, cream-coloured grubs weigh up to 150 g each.

HERCULES BEETLE LARVA

GIANT SAWYER BEETLE

GIANT SAWYER BEETLE

Giant sawyer beetles can reach nearly 18 cm long including a set of giant pincer-like jaws, which measure about 5 cm. The beetles use their jaws to chomp through wood, creating holes where they lay their eggs.

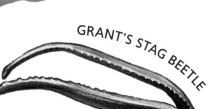
GRANT'S STAG BEETLE

GRANT'S STAG BEETLE

The jaws of a male Grant's stag beetle are as long as its body. Males battle each other on tree trunks, and use their jaws like tweezers to pick up their rivals and throw them off.

FEATHER-WINGED BEETLE

The tiniest beetles are among some of the smallest of all insects. Known as feather-winged beetles, these mini-beasts can be as small as 0.3 mm, and are found all over the world.

FEATHER-WINGED BEETLE, **too small to show life-size**

SILENT KILLER

Danger lurks in the dark, dank shadows of a tropical African forest. Hidden beneath the carpet of grown leaves lies the world's largest viper, the Gaboon viper. It reaches a terrifying 2 m long and weighs up to 10 kg. This silent killer is equipped with the longest fangs of any snake and deadly venom for poisoning its prey.

GABOON VIPER

The snake's head is a distinctive triangle shape, measuring up to 15 cm at its widest part.

KILLER INSTINCT

Gaboon vipers are ambush hunters, which means they lie in wait for something tasty to cross their path. When a viper spots a victim, its fangs rotate forwards. The snake opens its mouth wide – almost 180 degrees – lowering the fangs into place. It then plunges the fangs into its prey and injects venom deep into its tissues. A Gaboon viper usually stabs larger victims several times and then lets them go, watching and waiting for the venom to do its deadly work. This helps the snake avoid being injured during the attack. It keeps hold of smaller victims, waiting until they die.

BEAUTIFUL BEAST

Gaboon vipers are among the most beautiful of all snakes. Their scaly skin has a stunning pattern made up of rich browns. The colours and shapes help camouflage the snake, which blends invisibly into the forest floor. There it lies motionless until it can ambush prey. Gaboon vipers usually hunt

GLOSSARY

Here are explanations of some handy words.

Algae
A large group of plant-like organisms that mostly live in water.

Ambush
A surprise attack.

Arachnids
A group of animals without bones that have eight legs. Spiders, scorpions and mites are arachnids.

Bacteria
Tiny living things that are neither animals nor plants. Most exist as just one microscopic cell.

Camouflage
Colours, patterns and shapes on an animal's fur and skin that help it to hide in its environment.

Canopy
The top of a forest where most of the branches create a thick layer of leaves.

Carbon dioxide
A gas in the atmosphere. Animals breathe out carbon dioxide, and plants use it to photosynthesize and make their own food.

Climate
The pattern of weather that is typical of a place or region.

Courtship
A time when animals try to attract a mate.

Dispersal
The spreading of things over a wide area.

Environment
The surroundings where an organism lives, including climate vegetation and other living things.

Fang
A sharp, pointed tooth. Also called a canine tooth.

Fossilized
Turned into stone over a long period of time.

Global warming
The way that the planet's atmosphere is heating up, which is changing the world's climates.

Habitat
The place where an animal or plant naturally lives.

Insect
An animal without a backbone that, as an adult, has three pairs of legs. Beetles, flies and butterflies are insects.

Larva
A young, soft-bodied insect. Maggots, caterpillars and grubs are types of larvae.

Mammal
A type of vertebrate that feeds its young with milk and usually gives birth to babies, rather than laying eggs. Most mammals have hair or fur.

Moss
A small, slow-growing plant that usually grows in a cushion shape in damp habitats. Mosses do not have flowers.

Nectar
A sweet liquid made by flowers to attract insects. Bees use nectar to make honey and feed their larvae.

Nocturnal
Active at night instead of in the day.

Nutrients
Food, or parts of food, such as vitamins.

Nymph
A young insect that looks like the adult, but smaller.

Organism
A living thing. Plants, animals, fungi, bacteria and algae are all organisms.

Oxygen
A gas in the atmosphere that is produced by plants. Animals need oxygen to breathe and release energy from food.

Parasite
A living thing that lives on, or in, another organism and does it harm.

Photosynthesis
The process that plants use to make food. They use the energy from sunlight to turn carbon dioxide and water into food.

Plumage
A bird's feathers.

Pollinate
When pollen lands on the female part of a flower. The pollen will join with an egg and together they grow into a seed.

Predator
An animal that hunts other animals to eat.

Prey
An animal that is hunted by a predator.

Pupil
The dark part in the centre of an eye, where light enters.

Skull
The hard, bony case that protects an animal's brain.

Tissue
A group or layer of cells in an animal's body that have particular jobs to do, such as muscle or skin.

Toxic
Poisonous or harmful to a living thing.

Tropical
Something from the area around the Equator. The tropics typically have a warm, wet climate.

Venom
A type of poison that is usually injected with teeth, claws, stings or spines.

Vertebrate
An animal with a skeleton. Mammals, reptiles, birds, fish and amphibians are vertebrates.

Vine
A type of plant that climbs up other plants or trails along the ground.

Viper
A type of snake with large fangs that can fold up inside the snake's mouth.

UNITS OF MEASUREMENT

Here are some units of measurement used inside the book and what they've been abbreviated to.

millimetre: mm   gram: g
metre: m   kilogram: kg
centimetre: cm   tonne: t
kilometre: km   litre: L

IMPERIAL MEASUREMENTS

Here are the metric measurements from inside this book converted into imperial measurements.

1 micrometre: 0.000039 inches
1 millimetre: 0.04 inches
1 metre: 3.28 feet
1 centimetre: 0.39 inches
1 kilometre: 0.62 miles
1 kilometre per hour: 0.62 miles per hour
1 cubic metre: 264.17 US gallons
1 cubic kilometre: 0.24 cubic miles
1 milligram: 0.000035 ounces
1 gram: 0.04 ounces
1 kilogram: 2.2 pounds
1 tonne: 1.1 tons
1 litre: 1.76 pints